my Pennsylvania garden

a gardener's journal

Liz Ball

COOL SPRINGS PRESS

ISBN 1-930604-06-8

NOTE: The ideas expressed in this book are not, in all cases, exact quotations, as some have been edited to fit the format. In all cases, the publisher has attempted to maintain the speaker's original intent. Further, in some cases, source materials for this book were obtained from secondary sources, primarily print media and the Internet. While every effort has been made to ensure the accuracy of these sources, accuracy cannot be guaranteed. To notify us of any corrections or clarifications, please contact Cool Springs Press.

Cool Springs Press, Inc.
112 Second Avenue North
Franklin, TN 37064

First Printing 2000
Printed in the United States of America
10 9 8 7 6 5 4 3 2 1

Design by:	Sheri Ferguson
Illustrations by:	Allison Starcher
Editorial Consultant:	Erica Glasener

Visit the Cool Springs Press website at www.coolspringspress.com

my *Pennsylvania* garden

a gardener's journal

this is my

Pennsylvania

garden

_____
name

2004
year

why keep a garden journal ?

Welcome! We Pennsylvania gardeners are known for our boldness and enthusiasm. We realize gardening is a constant learning process. We have minds of our own—and sometimes it seems that our plants do too. That's why you need *My Pennsylvania Garden: A Gardener's Journal.*

Keeping a garden journal will help you keep track of how your garden grows. You will discover which plants thrive, which ones struggle, and best of all, you will discover many surprises. More than just record keeping, journaling is a way to trace your growth as a gardener. Writing down your favorite moments in the garden may help you decide which plants to add or which to replace. How does your garden make you feel? You may discover you prefer one season to another. Maybe your style of gardening has changed. A journal will help you track the evolution of your garden.

As gardeners know, weather is a huge factor in plant performance. By keeping track of air temperature, the amount of rainfall, and drastic changes (storms or droughts), we can see which plants survived and plan better for next year.

Has the environment in your garden changed? Trees and shrubs that were once small may have matured and created a shadier garden. Keeping a list of what you plant, where and when you plant it, and the source of the plant will provide useful information for the future.

Further, keeping up with what's blooming when, and how long it blooms is another reason to write daily or weekly in your garden journal. You might be surprised at how many times during the year your garden features beautiful blooms, colorful foliage, or fantastic fruits. Some of the best color combinations happen by accident and remembering which plant blooms and when it blooms from year to year is not easy. With good journal records, you may recreate pleasing plant combinations and avoid repeating mistakes.

How often you fertilize, prune, and water are other things to keep track of in your garden journal. Which techniques have been most successful? If you have a particular pest or disease problem with one plant, what methods were effective in eradicating or controlling the problem? If your roses were beautiful last year, when did you prune them and how much did you prune? When did you divide your daylilies and where did you plant the different kinds of spring bulbs? All of these questions can be answered in the pages of *My Pennyslyvania Garden.*

getting started with your garden journal

By keeping daily records, you can check your journal and chart your most successful garden practices. Whether it's how and when you propagated a favorite perennial, when the clematis first came into bloom, or when you noticed the scent of a particular narcissus, your Pennsylvania garden journal will provide the ideal format for keeping in touch with your garden and what it can teach you. Here's how to begin.

- Designate a day and a time during the week to write in your journal. You might discover that early morning coffee time or the end of the day works best.

- Use a favorite pen and keep it with your journal. Write brief, clear notes (*rainy and cool with temp around 60° F, Phlox 'David' has been in bloom for 2 weeks, Rose of Sharon loaded with flower buds, planted two hardy geraniums in perennial garden, 'Johnson's Blue' and 'Claridge Druce', purchased from the specialty nursery in Oregon*).

- Keep a 5"x7" envelope tucked in the back of your journal to hold photographs and pictures from catalogs or magazines that inspire you. Be sure to identify and label pictures.

- List existing trees, shrubs, perennials, and bulbs and include a sketch of where they are located. This will be especially helpful over the years when you make changes in your garden.

    Once you get used to journaling, you may find that you look forward to writing about your garden as much as you enjoy adding new plants.

Growing plants has always been part of life in Pennsylvania because our unique location and climate has made it relatively easy. Situated between the nation's northern and southern extremes of temperature, our state has been blessed with thick forests which built and protected excellent soil and moderated the climate over the eons.

The earliest Dutch, Swedish, then English, settlers immediately recognized that farming would be successful here. Then, spurred by their Enlightenment enthusiasm and curiosity about natural science and plants, William Penn and his followers made Philadelphia a wellspring of horticultural knowledge and activity. This horticultural tradition was embraced by successive waves of immigrants, such as the Amish in Lancaster County, who pushed westward across the Commonwealth tilling the soil and harvesting its bounty as they went.

Pennsylvania's topography is marked by the gently rolling Piedmont region in the eastern part of the state. It yields toward the west to the Allegheny Mountains which parade across the vast central portion of the state over to the Allegheny plateau near Pittsburgh. Climatic conditions vary over these regions, especially winter cold. In the system of cold hardiness zones developed and defined by the USDA, most of Pennsylvania falls in zones 5 and 6. A small area south of Philadelphia is a relatively mild zone 7. These zone designations are based on the average annual minimum temperature of an area, with each zone number indicating a difference of 10 degrees. The lower the number, the colder the winters. Knowing which zone you live in is a helpful guide to choosing and caring for plants.

choosing plants

Because so many plants do well in Pennsylvania, it is difficult to decide which ones to choose for your yard and garden. A good place to start is by eliminating those that are not labeled for your area's hardiness zone. Although every home landscape has unique features that create warmer or more sheltered areas—micro-climates where less hardy plants may do well—it is a good idea to use the official zones as guidelines for perennial plants that must survive winter. Later, as you observe the seasons in your yard, prevailing air flow, sunlight, and moisture patterns, experiment with some marginally hardy plants.

There are several issues that influence the choice of plants for most homeowners. One is the desire for diversity. Not only is a variety of types and kinds of plants more attractive, it also creates a healthier overall environment. Lots of different plants support lots of beneficial creatures to carry out pollination and pest control. The more plant species, the better the balance of pest and predator. A related issue is wildlife habitat. As suburban development fragments the Pennsylvania wilderness and deprives wildlife of food and shelter, backyards can help replace them. Choose plants that bear berries, cones, and seeds for birds and other small mammals. Plants that are native to Pennsylvania do the best job. Another issue is choosing plants for a practical purpose such as screening out noise or a view, blocking winter wind to save on heating bills, or preventing soil erosion on a steep hill. Perhaps you want plants that are fragrant or good for shearing as hedges or for cut flowers. If this all seems too overwhelming, consider hiring a professional landscape designer to help you analyze your property, soil, and goals.

preparing for plants

After choosing a site that offers the right sun or shade, the most important thing you can do for your plants is to give them good soil. Since most soil in Pennsylvania is somewhat acidic, a pH test is likely to confirm that it is fine for most plants. An inexpensive pH meter with a probe that you stick into the soil will register any major deviation from the desirable range of 5.5 to 7.0. Chances are, though, if azaleas, rhododendron, and hollies are doing well in your yard, the soil may be a bit too acidic for the lawn.

In our state, homeowners routinely spread lime on lawns in the fall every couple of years to "sweeten" the soil for northern turfgrasses. It provides calcium too, which all plants need.

It is hard to know just by looking at soil whether it is nutritious or fertile. The major nutrients, nitrogen (N), phosphorus (P), and potassium (K) must not only be present, but they should be in the right proportion. The best way to determine this information is by a soil test done by a laboratory. Kits for the test are available from your county Agricultural Extension office. Instructions are enclosed. Test results mailed to you will indicate things like amounts of nutrients, nutrient deficiencies, pH imbalance, and how to correct them.

Handling your soil is the best way to determine its texture. The best soil both drains well and retains moisture because it has lots of spongy humus in it. Improve thin or clay soil by mixing in organic matter in the form of homemade or municipal compost, peat moss, or chopped leaves. Spread a thin layer as a topdressing on the lawn to improve soil under the turf. Periodically, core aerate the lawn and dig in established beds to reduce compaction and introduce air into the soil. The oxygen supports essential microbial life, worms, and other natural residents that process nutrients for plants.

keeping plants happy

The key to success with plants is to keep them happy—supplying nutritious, aerated soil, sufficient moisture, appropriate light, and support if needed. If they are not stressed, they can handle most insect and disease problems. Sometimes a change in their environment, such as drought, the removal of a tree that gave shade, or pollution of some sort unavoidably compromises their health. You may correct the situation by moving the plant or watering. Occasionally, environmental stress causes a population explosion of some pest, which overwhelms the vulnerable plant. It may be necessary to pinch or hose off the bugs or spot spray an insecticide on them to reduce the infestation until the plant recovers.

fertilizing

Over the years, even the most fertile soil is depleted of nutrients if organic matter is not regularly added to the soil. This is particularly true in gardens where plants must constantly produce flowers, seeds, or fruits for harvest and in lawns where plants must constantly regenerate their foliage due to repeated mowing. Provide consistent, uniform nutrition to your home landscape by using a general purpose, slow-acting, granular fertilizer at the beginning of the growing season. Whether it is organic or synthesized, its nitrogen (N), phosphorus (P) and potassium (K) will remain available to plant roots consistently over many weeks. If your soil test reveals an imbalance of these major nutrients, then temporarily use a product which features a greater proportion of the one you need. This is indicated on the label in words and by a series of three numbers indicating the ratio of N, P, and K. Avoid overfertilizing plants indoors or outside. Insects and diseases love the excessive tender new growth that a rich diet promotes.

watering

Pennsylvania has historically had generous rainfall. However, in recent years, weather patterns have changed everywhere, and ours is no exception. The best insurance against the type of drought we had in the summer of 1999 is to install a drip irrigation system in beds planted with shrubs, trees, ornamental, and food plants. It delivers water most efficiently and effectively for healthier plants and water conservation. Standard hose sprinklers are fine for lawns during brief drought periods. During longer droughts, it is healthier for northern grasses to go dormant than to be intermittently watered. Most outdoor plants will need about 1 inch of water per week, either from rainfall or irrigation. Plants in containers in the sun will need more water, especially in the summer.

mulching

Spread a 2- or 3-inch layer of organic material such as chopped leaves, pine needles, or commercial bark product over all the bare soil under and between plants on your property. This is how nature protects and renews the soil in the wild. In planted beds, organic mulch discourages weeds and helps the soil retain moisture. As it decomposes in the hot weather it also contributes humus and microbial life to the soil to keep it healthy. Stubborn perennial weeds may require hand or mechanical pulling or a spot treatment with a safe soap or glysophate-based herbicide. As the mulch layer becomes thin over the season, add more, but never pile it up against plant stems. In the winter, mulch insulates soil to protect it from alternate freezing and thawing which disturbs plants, especially bulbs.

grooming

Supervise the development of your plants to keep them sturdy and healthy. Thin young ones if they become too crowded. Guide their growth and shape by erecting supports for those that threaten to flop in wind or rain. Keeping certain flowers and vegetables off of the ground protects them from disease and provides them with better light and air circulation. Some plants such as impatiens, basil, and chrysanthemums benefit from pinching back stems to make them bushier and more compact. Others such as tomatoes form stronger stems and larger fruit or flowers if subsidiary branchlets, called suckers, are routinely clipped off. Removing faded flowers before they form seeds, called deadheading, promotes continued blooming for many flowering annuals, as well as some perennials. Proper pruning of woody vines, trees, and shrubs improves their access to light and air, stimulates their growth, helps them heal properly, and prevents disease and insect problems.

Pennsylvania Garden Favorites

I selected a list of plants that are easy to grow, readily available, adaptable to various growing conditions in Pennsylvania, and which help provide year-round interest. These plants can be very beneficial to your Pennsylvania yard and garden because they provide brilliant color, some attract birds and wildlife, and most require minimal maintenance. You will find information on these and other recommendations in my book, *The Philadelphia Garden Book* (Cool Springs Press, 1999). Give these a try!

Annuals

- Coleus — *Solenostemon scutellarioides*
- Cosmos — *Cosmos bipinnatus*
- Geranium — *Pelargonium* x *hortorum*
- Impatiens —
  Impatiens wallerana 'Busy Lizzie'
- Marigold — *Tagetes* species and hybrids

- Nasturtium — *Tropaeolum majus*
- Pansy — *Viola* x *wittrockiana*
- Petunia — *Petunia* x *hybrida*
- Spider Flower — *Cleome hasslerana*
- Sunflower — *Helianthus annum*

Perennials

- Artemisia —
  Artemisia species and hybrid
- Beebalm — *Monarda didyma*
- Black-Eyed Susan —
  Rudbeckia fulgida sullivantii
  'Goldsturm'
- Bleeding Heart — *Dicentra exemia*
- Coralbells — *Heuchera sanguinea*

- Chrysanthemum, Garden —
  Chrysanthemum x *morifolium*
- Coreopsis — *Coreopsis lanceolata*
- Daylily —
  Hemerocallis species and hybrids
- Goldenrod —
  Solidago species and hybrids
- Hosta — *Hosta* species and hybrids

Bulbs

- Begonia, Tuberous —
  Begonia x *tuberhybrida*
- Canna — *Canna* x *generalis*
- Crocus — *Crocus vernus*
- Daffodil — *Narcissus* species and hybrids
- Dahlia — *Dahlia* species and hybrids

- Gladiolus — *Gladiolus* x *hortulanus*
- Iris, Bearded — *Iris germanica*
- Lily — *Lilium* species and hybrids
- Onion, Ornamental —
  Allium aflatunense 'Globemaster'
- Tulip — *Tulipa* species and hybrids

Aquatic plants

- Cattail — *Typha angustifolia*
- Lotus — *Nelumbo nucifera*
- Papyrus — *Cyperus* species
- Parrot's Feather —
  Myriophyllum aquaticum
- Pickerel Rush — *Pontederia cordata*

- Taro — *Colocasia esculenta*
- Thalia — *Thalia dealbata*
- Water Hyacinth — *Eichhornia crassipes*
- Water Lily — *Nymphaea* species
- Yellow Flag — *Iris pseudacorus*

Vines

- Boston Ivy — *Parthenocissus tricuspidata*
- Clematis — *Clematis* hybrids
- Climbing Hydrangea — *Hydrangea anomala petiolaris*
- Hyacinth Bean — *Dolichos lablab*
- Kiwi — *Actinidia kolomitka*
- Moonflower — *Ipomoea alba*
- Scarlet Honeysuckle — *Lonicera sempervirens*
- Wisteria — *Wisteria floribunda*

Trees

- Bald Cypress — *Taxodium distichum*
- Birch, River — *Betula nigra* 'Heritage'
- Falsecypress, Hinoki — *Chamaecyparis obtusa*
- Ginkgo — *Ginkgo biloba*
- Holly, American — *Ilex opaca*
- Linden, Littleleaf — *Tilia cordata*
- Magnolia, Saucer — *Magnolia x soulangiana*
- Maple, Japanese — *Acer palmatum*
- Oak, White — *Quercus alba*
- Sourwood — *Oxydendrum arboreum*

Shrubs

- Azalea, Evergreen — *Rhododendron* species and hybrids
- Barberry, Japanese — *Berberis thunbergii*
- Butterfly Bush — *Buddleia davidii*
- Hydrangea, Oakleaf — *Hydrangea quercifolia*
- Mountain Laurel — *Kalmia latifolia*
- Rhododendron — *Rhododendron* species and hybrids
- Shadblow — *Amelanchier canadensis*
- Shrub Rose — *Rosa* species and hybrids
- Viburnum, Doublefile — *Viburnum plicatum*
- Virginia Sweetspire — *Itea virginica*

Ground covers

- Ajuga — *Ajuga reptans*
- Barrenwort — *Epimedium grandiflorum*
- Creeping Phlox — *Phlox stolonifera*
- Deadnettle — *Lamium maculatum*
- English Ivy — *Hedera helix*
- Foamflower — *Tiarella cordifolia*
- Japanese Painted Fern — *Athyrium nipponicum* 'Pictum'
- Lamb's Ears — *Stachys byzantina*
- Lilyturf — *Liriope spicata*
- Moneywort — *Lysimachia nummularia* 'Aurea'

Ornamental grasses

- Blue Fescue — *Festuca ovina* 'Glauca'
- Fountaingrass — *Pennisetum* species
- Hakonechloa — *Hakonechloa macra* 'Aureola'
- Maiden Grass — *Miscanthus sinensis*
- Switch Grass — *Panicum virgatum*

Turf grasses

- Kentucky Bluegrass — *Poa pratensis*
- Perennial Ryegrass — *Lolium perenne*
- Tall Fescue — *Festuca elatior*

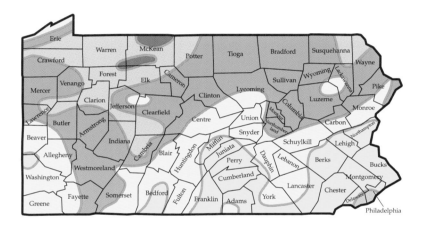

Average Annual Minimum Temperature

4B	-20° F to -25° F
5A	-15° F to -20° F
5B	-10° F to -15° F
6A	-5° F to -10° F
6B	0° F to -5° F
7A	5° F to 0° F

*To create a
little flower is the
labour of ages.*

— *William Blake*

January

garden observations

what's the weather like?

Start the year off right! Photograph your garden at least once every month. This will help you with your planning and planting schemes.

what have I planted/transplanted?

garden notes

What is a weed? A plant whose virtues have not yet been dicovered.

— Ralph Waldo Emerson

January

garden observations

Order seeds now for your favorite annuals, perennials and vegetables. Cut out color photographs and create your own record for what you order.

what's the weather like?

When planning your garden, use a large sheet of graph paper with 1/4 inch grids. A scale of 1 inch = 4 feet is a useful proportion.

what have I planted/transplanted?

garden notes

January

garden observations

what's the weather like?

what have I planted/transplanted?

Check house plants for signs of insects and disease. Spots, speckles or webs on leaves indicate pests are present.

January

garden observations

what's the weather like?

Tip to Remember:
You may also use
vegetables as
ornamental plants.
Ornamental peppers
and sweet potato vine
selections are good
examples.

what have I planted/transplanted?

garden notes

February

garden observations

what's the weather like?

Take a walk through your garden, and plan additions to create winter interest for next year.

what have I planted/transplanted?

Did You Know? The only tulip color that has not yet been developed is any shade of blue.

garden notes

february | week 1

February

garden observations

what's the weather like?

When in doubt,
call your local
Extension Service.
Master Gardeners
there will provide
information (and
the advice is free!)

what have I planted/transplanted?

garden notes

February

garden observations

Extend the life of your cut flowers. Remove the lower leaves and re-cut the stems before arranging them in lukewarm water.

what's the weather like?

what have I planted/transplanted?

Though I do not believe
that a plant will spring
up where no seed has been,
I have great faith in a
seed. Convince me that
you have a seed there,
and I am prepared to
expect wonders.

—Henry David Thoreau

garden observations

what's the weather like?

Tip to Remember:
Fill clear plastic
milk jugs with
water and place
around young
tomato plants.
They will provide
warmth overnight
for young plants,
helping you get a
jump on spring.

what have I planted/transplanted?

march | week 1

March

what's blooming?

Direct sow wildflower
seeds where you want
them to grow in
climates with USDA
zones 1 through 6.
(Check the zone map
in the introduction to
identify your zone.)

what's the weather like?

Take a soil test now
so you will know how
to prepare your garden
for the next season.

what have I planted/transplanted?

garden notes

march | week 1

March

what's blooming?

Tip to Remember:
Plan to add a few
annuals to your
perennial garden
to help provide
season-long blooms.

what's the weather like?

Watch for aphids on
shrubs as they leaf out.
Treat with insecticidal
soap or any other
labeled pesticide,
if needed.

what have I planted/transplanted?

Start tomato seeds for
transplants 4-6 weeks
before optimum plant-
ing time in your area.

garden notes

march | week 3

March

what's blooming?

Single-flower forms of
marigolds and zinnias
are more appealing to
butterflies than the
double-flower forms.

what's the weather like?

Did You Know?
Viburnum is a
member of the
honeysuckle family.

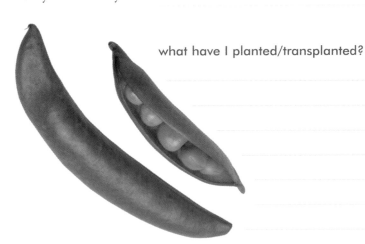

what have I planted/transplanted?

garden notes

march | week 3

March

what's blooming?

what's the weather like?

Hummingbirds love
tubular flowers such
as trumpet vine, coral
honeysuckle, and
nicotiana. Plant lots
of these if you want to
attract hummingbirds.

what have I planted/transplanted?

garden notes

Half the interest of a garden is the constant exercise of the imagination.

— C.W. Earle

april week 1

what's blooming?

what's the weather like?

Have you
photographed
your garden lately?
This will help with
your garden planning
and design ideas.

what have I planted/transplanted?

An easy time to weed
is the day after a
gentle rain, when the
soil is slightly moist,
and weeds are easy to
pull—roots and all.

tending my garden

april | week 1

Propagate some
of your favorite
broadleaf shrubs using
this simple layering
technique: Select a
branch that is close to
the ground. Bend the
branch so that it is in
contact with the soil.
Cover the branch
with soil. Water well
and hold the branch
in place with a brick.
In six weeks, check to
see if there are roots.
Once the roots are
firmly established,
cut the new plant
off from the
mother plant.

what's the weather like?

what have I planted/transplanted?

As is the gardener, such
is the garden.

— Hebrew Proverb

april | week 3

what's blooming?

Tip to Remember:
When digging a hole
for a tree, it's best to
dig the hole at least
half again as wide as
the size of the rootball
(much wider is even
better). Use the same
soil you dug out to
backfill around
the rootball and
water-in well.

what's the weather like?

Turn your compost
pile. If you haven't
started one already,
call your Extension
Service for advice.

what have I planted/transplanted?

a p r i l week 4

Wooden clothespins
can be used as plant
markers.

Place grow-thru stakes
above plants that need
support in early
spring, and in a
short time they will
cover the stakes.

may week 1

May

Plan to prune back spring-blooming azaleas and other shrubs such as forsythia or spirea after they finish flowering. This way you won't cut off any potential flower buds for next year.

Check plants once or twice a week for insect and disease problems. It's easier to control a small infestation if it's discovered early.

what's blooming?

what's the weather like?

what have I planted/transplanted?

garden notes

may week 2

May

what's blooming?

what's the weather like?

Incorporate a
slow-release fertilizer
in the soil of hanging
baskets and container
plantings. This will
provide nutrients for
several months in
one application.

what have I planted/transplanted?

garden notes

Many diseases
can be controlled
with sanitation.
Remove and destroy
any infected leaves
as soon as they
are found.

may | week 2

May

what's blooming?

what's the weather like?

Parsley and fennel
provide food for
butterfly caterpillars.

Interest children
in gardening by
planning a small
child's garden. A
bean tee-pee is fun
to plant and grow!

what have I planted/transplanted?

garden notes

The best time
for slug hunting
is at night using
a flashlight and
a pair of gloves.

may | week 3

may week 4

May

what's blooming?

what's the weather like?

what have I planted/transplanted?

garden notes

*Tickle it with a hoe
and it will laugh
into a harvest.*

—English Proverb

june week 1

June

A perennial garden looks wonderful when planted against a background of a wall, a hedge, or evergreen shrubs.

A plant's scientific name consists of a genus and an epithet. The genus and the epithet are always italicized and the genus begins with a capital letter. A third word in the name may refer to a specific variety, called a cultivar. It is set off by single quotation marks.

what's blooming?

what's the weather like?

what have I planted/transplanted?

garden notes

june | week 1

june week 2

June

what's blooming?

Use vines to create vertical interest in the garden. If you don't have a wall or fence on which to train them, a lattice or arbor will work.

what's the weather like?

You can create your own portable seep irrigation system by punching a few holes in plastic containers and placing them beside plants that need additional moisture.

what have I planted/transplanted?

garden notes

Though an old man,
I am but a young
gardener...

— Thomas Jefferson

june | week 3

June

Plan to shear fall-blooming asters to make them bushier and more compact.

what's blooming?

what's the weather like?

Did You Know?
Even though a plant may be identified as self-cleaning, flowers are better off if you deadhead, or remove the spent blooms as often as you can. This will allow the plant to use its energy to make more flowers and leaves instead of making seeds.

what have I planted/transplanted?

june | week 4

what's blooming?

what's the weather like?

BTK (*Bacillus thuringiensis kurstaki*) is an organic biological control that is effective against many caterpillars and is safe to use on vegetable crops. *Bacillus thuringiensis* 'San Diego' is effective against some leafeating beetles.

what have I planted/transplanted?

garden notes

july week 1

July

Harvest herbs for drying as soon as they come into flower. Bundle them up with a rubber band and hang them on a line in a dark, dry place with good air circulation. To preserve the best flavor once they are dry, store the herbs in airtight containers away from heat and light.

Press some flowers and add to this journal. It's a pretty record of what you planted.

what's blooming?

what's the weather like?

what have I planted/transplanted?

garden notes

july | week 1

july week 2

what's blooming?

what's the weather like?

what have I planted/transplanted?

Deadhead hybrid tea roses throughout the summer to encourage more blooms.

garden notes

july week 3

July

what's blooming?

_____

_____

_____

_____

_____

_____

what's the weather like?

_____

_____

_____

_____

Most unwanted summer heat comes through east- and west-facing windows, not through well-insulated roofs and walls. Plant a deciduous tree for shade.

what have I planted/transplanted?

_____

_____

_____

_____

garden notes

what's blooming?

Plants use calcium
to build strong cell
walls and stems.
Deficiencies can
cause blossom-end
rot on tomatoes.

what's the weather like?

Did You Know? The
Greeks and Romans
used lavender in bath
water. In fact, the
Latin name "lavare"
means, "wash".

Tip to Remember:
When planting seeds,
position them in
geometric patterns so
that you will be able
to distinguish them
more easily from
weed seedlings.

what have I planted/transplanted?

garden notes

*Gardening is the purest
of human pleasures.*

— Francis Bacon

what's blooming?

what's the weather like?

Preserve basil leaves by mixing them in the blender with a small amount of water. Fill ice cube trays with the mix-ture. Once they freeze, put them in freezer bags. This way you will have basil to use in your favorite Italian dishes all winter long.

what have I planted/transplanted?

august | week 1

August

what's blooming?

For the best
selection, order your
spring-flowering bulbs
or purchase them
locally when they
become available in
your area. Keep them
cool and dry until
you plant them.

what's the weather like?

Take some
photographs of
your garden to refer
to later when plan-
ning for next year.

what have I planted/transplanted?

If you haven't already done so, draw a plan of your property showing existing trees and shrubs in relation to your house. Make notes throughout the year indicating those areas that receive full sun, shade or a mix of sun and shade. This will help you to choose the right plant for the right place.

what's blooming?

what's the weather like?

what have I planted/transplanted?

august | week 4

August

what's blooming?

Water your compost
pile when the weather
has been dry.

what's the weather like?

Order three or four
types of paperwhite
narcissus to force at
two-week intervals.
You will have flowers
from Halloween into
the New Year!

what have I planted/transplanted?

Continue to harvest
vegetables as soon as
they are ripe. Regular
harvesting increases
production.

garden notes

*He who plants
a garden plants
happiness.*
— Chinese Proverb

september

what's blooming?

what's the weather like?

Expand your plant
collection by exchang-
ing seeds and plants
with fellow gardeners.

what have I planted/transplanted?

Add some shrubs to
your garden that will
offer winter interest
such as colorful bark,
or unusual shapes.

garden notes

what's blooming?

what's the weather like?

If you haven't started one already, begin a compost pile and let it overwinter. In six months you should have "black gold" to mix into your garden.

what have I planted/transplanted?

garden notes

The frost hurts not weeds.

— Thomas Fuller

september

what's blooming?

what's the weather like?

what have I planted/transplanted?

If your annuals are beginning to look ragged, pull them and replace with some mums, pansies, or flowering kale.

september | week 4

september

what's blooming?

Use dried seed
heads such as sedum
and lotus for fall
decorations.

Visit your favorite
nursery to select a tree
or shrub for that spot
in the garden that
needs something new.

what's the weather like?

what have I planted/transplanted?

garden notes

what's blooming?

what's the weather like?

Plant a tree in honor
of a birth or in
memory of a
loved one.

Fall leaf color is trig-
gered by cooler tem-
peratures, shorter
days, and less light.

what have I planted/transplanted?

tending my garden

october | week 1

October

what's blooming?

what's the weather like?

what have I planted/transplanted?

Sprinkle annual rye grass seed on top of the soil of pots you are forcing. By the time the bulbs bloom, it will create a green carpet underneath them.

october | week 3

what's blooming?

what's the weather like?

Tip to Remember:
Parsley is a good
plant for bed edges.
It also looks great
grown in containers
with pansies.

what have I planted/transplanted?

Use golf tees to mark
areas where bulbs are
planted.

*Heaven is under our feet
as well as over our heads.*

— Henry David Thoreau

october

what's blooming?

what's the weather like?

Did You Know?
The word 'wort',
as in St. John's Wort,
is an old English
term that means
"medicinal plant".

what have I planted/transplanted?

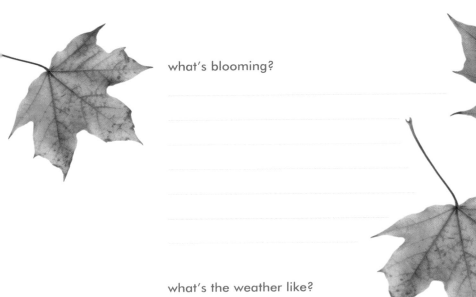

what's blooming?

what's the weather like?

Fall is the best time
to direct sow wild-
flower seeds in
USDA zones 7-9.
(Check the map in
the introduction to
verify your zone.)

what have I planted/transplanted?

garden notes

Autumn is a second spring when every leaf is a flower. —Albert Camus

november | week 2

November

what's blooming?

what's the weather like?

Continue to mow
your lawn for as long
as it keeps growing.

Clean and sharpen
garden tools. Lightly
coat with oil to
prevent rust.

what have I planted/transplanted?

what's blooming?

what's the weather like?

what have I planted/transplanted?

Extend the life of
your fresh-cut holiday
tree by storing it in a
cool shady place until
you move it indoors.
Re-cut the trunk
before moving it
indoors and use
plenty of fresh water
in the reservoir.

November

what's blooming?

For best results, store
unused seeds in a
cool, dark place in
an air- and water-
resistant container.

what's the weather like?

Selecting the right
tool for the job can
prevent most injuries.
Wear safety gear
when operating
power equipment.

what have I planted/transplanted?

December

garden observations

Make a wreath for the holidays. Rose hips, bittersweet, and euonymus are good choices for materials.

what's the weather like?

what have I planted/ transplanted?

*A garden is a friend
you can visit any time.*

— unknown

December

garden observations

Cast iron plant, Chinese evergreen, heartleaf philodendron, and snake plant will tolerate low-light conditions.

what's the weather like?

Tip to Remember: The winter sun provides the most solar heat through south-facing windows. Avoid planting shade trees or evergreens that may shade these heat-absorbing windows if you need the extra warmth.

what have I planted/transplanted?

garden notes

December

garden observations

Recycle your holiday tree. The branches can be removed and used as mulch. Or you can leave the tree intact and use it as a windbreak and shelter for birds.

what's the weather like?

Don't put wood ashes in your compost pile; they will alter the pH level too much.

what have I planted/transplanted?

garden notes

december | week 4

December

garden observations

what's the weather like?

what have I planted/transplanted?

garden notes

Pruning large trees,
especially those located
near utilities should
be performed by a
professional. Call a
certified arborist if you
need trees pruned.

plant inventory/history

name

when planted

where planted

size

source

price

name

when planted

where planted

size

source

price

name

when planted

where planted

size

source

price

name

when planted

where planted

size

source

price

name

when planted

where planted

size

source

price

name

when planted

where planted

size

source

price

name

when planted

where planted

size

source

price

name

when planted

where planted

size

source

price

name

when planted

where planted

size

source

price

name

when planted

where planted

size

source

price

name

when planted

where planted

size

source

price

name

when planted

where planted

size

source

price

name

when planted

where planted

size

source

price

name

when planted

where planted

size

source

price

name

when planted

where planted

size

source

price

name

when planted

where planted

size

source

price

plant inventory/history

name

when planted

where planted

size

source

price

name

when planted

where planted

size

source

price

name

when planted

where planted

size

source

price

name

when planted

where planted

size

source

price

name

when planted

where planted

size

source

price

name

when planted

where planted

size

source

price

name

when planted

where planted

size

source

price

name

when planted

where planted

size

source

price

name

when planted

where planted

size

source

price

name

when planted

where planted

size

source

price

name

when planted

where planted

size

source

price

name

when planted

where planted

size

source

price

name

when planted

where planted

size

source

price

name

when planted

where planted

size

source

price

name

when planted

where planted

size

source

price

name

when planted

where planted

size

source

price

plant inventory/history

name

when planted

where planted

size

source

price

name

when planted

where planted

size

source

price

name

when planted

where planted

size

source

price

name

when planted

where planted

size

source

price

name

when planted

where planted

size

source

price

name

when planted

where planted

size

source

price

name

when planted

where planted

size

source

price

name

when planted

where planted

size

source

price

name

when planted

where planted

size

source

price

name

when planted

where planted

size

source

price

name

when planted

where planted

size

source

price

name

when planted

where planted

size

source

price

name

when planted

where planted

size

source

price

name

when planted

where planted

size

source

price

name

when planted

where planted

size

source

price

name

when planted

where planted

size

source

price

plant inventory/history

name

when planted

where planted

size

source

price

name

when planted

where planted

size

source

price

name

when planted

where planted

size

source

price

name

when planted

where planted

size

source

price

name

when planted

where planted

size

source

price

name

when planted

where planted

size

source

price

name

when planted

where planted

size

source

price

name

when planted

where planted

size

source

price

name

when planted

where planted

size

source

price

name

when planted

where planted

size

source

price

name

when planted

where planted

size

source

price

name

when planted

where planted

size

source

price

name

when planted

where planted

size

source

price

name

when planted

where planted

size

source

price

name

when planted

where planted

size

source

price

name

when planted

where planted

size

source

price

my garden plan

suppliers & resources

photos